Praise for *The Sign of the Cross*

"As we accumulate years, the movement of grace most often challenges us to unclutter our life in God. The invitation is not to search for what is trendy and novel but to dive deeper into the tried and true. Bert Ghezzi's short but immensely rich *Sign of the Cross* leads us to do just that. This simplest of prayers that most of us learned as children calls us at every repetition to enter into the heart of our Baptism and claim the power of the cross and Resurrection right where we are. What could be more grace-filled and powerful than that?"

—**Fr. Brad A. Milunski**, OFM Conv., Rector, Basilica of St. Stanislaus, Chicopee, Massachusetts

"In his inimitable way, bestselling author Bert Ghezzi examines what seems to be a small, humble thing and reveals it to be in fact an immense, magnificent thing. *The Sign of the Cross* connects the dots for us between a familiar sacramental and a number of beautiful, powerful aspects of our life with God. Read this book, and you'll come to treasure in a whole new way this ancient and profound gesture of faith."

—**Paul Thigpen**, author of *The Life of Saint Joseph as Seen by the Mystics*

"Bert Ghezzi has placed the jewel of the prayer of the sign of the cross in a setting that reveals its beauty, inspiration, and holy energy."

—**Fr. Alfred McBride**, O. Praem., author of *Essentials of the Faith* and *Images of Jesus*

"Though brief in pages, this book is long on wisdom and insight. It deepened my experience of praying the sign of the cross."
—**Johnette Benkovic Williams**, EWTN host and Founder and Director of Women of Grace

"Bert Ghezzi's insights into the spiritual life are often shrewd, and his enthusiasm for this 'easy spiritual discipline' may prove to be contagious—powerfully so."
—*First Things*

"A helpful handbook for readers eager to explore their own spiritual practice more deeply. Readers already interested in the subject, particularly those from liturgical traditions, will find Ghezzi's combination of biblical scholarship, Church tradition, and common sense both informative and appealing."
—*Publishers Weekly*

"Using Scripture, Church teachings, and his own prayer life, Ghezzi describes how the sign of the cross offers an opening to God, a renewal of Baptism, a mark of discipleship, an acceptance of suffering, a defense against the devil, and a victory over self-indulgence."
—*Notre Dame Magazine*

"In this helpful resource, Bert Ghezzi, a Catholic writer, discusses the meaning of making the sign of the cross according to Scripture, Church teaching, the writings of the Church Fathers, the testimony of the saints, theology books, and his own personal experience."
—*Spirituality and Health*

THE SIGN OF THE
CROSS

THE SIGN OF THE
CROSS

Recovering the Power of the
Ancient Prayer

Bert Ghezzi

Published by Word on Fire,
Elk Grove Village, IL 60007
© 2023 by Bert Ghezzi
Printed in the United States of America
All rights reserved

Cover design, typesetting, and interior art direction by Marlene Burell and Rozann Lee

Except where otherwise indicated, all Scripture passages are taken from *The New Jerusalem Bible*, Doubleday Standard Edition, copyright © 1985 and 1999 by Doubleday, a division of Random House, Inc., and Darton, Longman & Todd, Ltd. Used by permission. Scripture passages marked RSV are taken from *The Revised Standard Version of the Bible*, copyright © 1946, 1952, 1971, by the Division of Christian Education of the National Council of Churches of Christ in the U.S.A. Used by permission. Scripture passages marked NRSV are taken from *New Revised Standard Version Bible*, copyright © 1989, by the Division of Christian Education of the National Council of Churches of Christ in the U.S.A. Used by permission. Scripture passages marked NIV are taken from the *Holy Bible, New International Version*.® Copyright © 1973, 1978, 1984 by International Bible Society. Used by permission of Zondervan Publishing House. The "NIV" and "New International Version" trademarks are registered in the United States Patent and Trademark Office by International Bible Society. Use of either trademark requires the permission of International Bible Society.

Excerpts from the English translation of the *Catechism of the Catholic Church* for use in the United States of America Copyright © 1994, United States Catholic Conference, Inc.—Libreria Editrice Vaticana. Used by permission. English translation of the *Catechism of the Catholic Church*: Modifications from the Editio Typica copyright © 1997, United States Conference of Catholic Bishops—Libreria Editrice Vaticana.

No part of this book may be used or reproduced in any manner whatsoever without written permission, except in the case of brief quotations in critical articles or reviews. For more information, contact Word on Fire, PO Box 170, Des Plaines, IL 60016 or email contact@wordonfire.org.

First Edition published 2006 by Loyola Press. Second Edition 2023.

26 25 24 23   1 2 3 4
ISBN: 978-1-68578-032-6
Library of Congress Control Number: 2022911945

One of the reasons why Infinite Wisdom has chosen the Cross is because a slight motion of the hand is sufficient to trace upon us the instrument of the divine torture: bright and powerful Sign, which teaches us all that we have to know, and serves as a buckler against our enemies.[1]

—ST. ALCUIN OF YORK (735–804)

CONTENTS

CHAPTER ONE
Recovering the Power of the Ancient Sign

But as for me, it is out of the question that I should boast of anything at all, except of the cross of our Lord Jesus Christ, through whom the world has been crucified to me and I to the world. . . . After this, let no one trouble me; I carry branded on my body the marks of Jesus.

—GALATIANS 6:14, 17

This sign is a powerful protection. It is gratuitous, because of the poor. Easy because of the weak. A benefit from God, the standard of the faithful, the terror of demons.[1]

—ST. CYRIL OF JERUSALEM (c. 315–386)

Adorn and protect each of your members with this victorious sign, and nothing can injure you.[2]

—ST. EPHREM THE SYRIAN (306–373)

✠

Aleksandr Solzhenitsyn leaned on his shovel and watched the gray clouds that dragged sullenly across the sky. A merciless wind tore at him through his prison garb. He felt as though it penetrated to his soul. Every bone and muscle ached. Hunger gnawed his stomach. Years of hard labor in the Siberian work camp had ruined his health and stripped him of hope.

Solzhenitsyn could endure no longer. He dropped his shovel, left the work gang, and sat on a bench nearby. Soon a guard would command him to return to work. When he would ignore the order, the guard would beat him to death, probably with his own shovel. He had seen it happen to others many times. *A quick, bloody death today*, thought Solzhenitsyn, *would be better than a slow death in a bleak and empty future.*

He stared at the ground, waiting for the inevitable. Soon he heard footsteps and braced himself in anticipation of the guard's harsh words. But when he raised his eyes, instead of a guard, he saw a gaunt, elderly prisoner standing before him. The old man said nothing, but knelt in front of Solzhenitsyn. With a stick he scratched the sign of the cross in the dirt and hurried back to work.

Solzhenitsyn looked at the cross and, as he reflected on it, a ray of light penetrated his dark thoughts. In that moment, his perspective changed radically. He realized that he did not have to face the evil of the gulag and the Soviets on his own diminished strength. With the power of the cross, he could withstand the evil of not just one but a thousand Soviet empires.

He got up from the bench and returned to work. Externally, none of Solzhenitsyn's oppressive circumstances changed that day, but internally he had experienced a gentle revolution. The sign of the cross had blessed him with the grace of hope.[3]

I found this story in an internet search, and it moved me deeply because it affirmed something I had been discovering in my own prayer. For some reason, in the past few years, I have taken the sign of the cross more seriously. I signed myself more frequently and with more reverence and faith. Over time I sensed that crossing myself tapped into a powerful divine energy that had many practical consequences for my life. It opened me to a flow of graces that strengthened me to face the challenges that arose every day.

When I reflected on how things were going for me, I realized that I was doing better with controlling my anger and overcoming other problems. I also felt that I was relating to God more freely and directly. I asked myself what I was doing differently that might account for this noticeable progress. The only answer I came up with was my praying more earnestly with the sign of the cross.

As I sought to understand what was happening to me, I read some articles and books about the sign of the cross.

A little research showed me that what was a novel experience for me had been the normal, everyday experience of Christians in the Church's first centuries. I learned that many early Christian writers described how believers signed themselves frequently. For example, Tertullian (c. 160–c. 240), a theologian writing at the turn of the third century, said, "In all our travels and movements, in all our coming in and going out, in putting on our shoes, at the bath, at the table, in lighting our candles, in lying down, in sitting down, whatever employment occupies us, we mark our foreheads with the sign of the cross."[4] And my reading showed further that the Fathers of the Church testified to the great blessings and power attached to the sign of the cross. I will quote them extensively throughout this book, but here I will cite only St. John Chrysostom (347–407), the eloquent fourth-century preacher and patriarch of Constantinople:

> Never leave your house without making the sign of the cross. It will be to you a staff, a weapon, an impregnable fortress. Neither man nor demon will dare to attack you, seeing you covered with such powerful armor. Let this sign teach you that you are a soldier, ready to combat against the demons, and ready to fight for the crown of justice. Are you ignorant of what the cross has done? It has vanquished death, destroyed sin, emptied hell, dethroned Satan, and restored the universe. Would you then doubt its power?[5]

When I was a little boy, my mother taught me to make the sign of the cross as I knelt for prayers at bedtime. For all the years since, I have signed myself at the start and close of my prayer. But in retrospect I realize that, while I have always used the gesture respectfully, I made it routinely, superficially, and unaware of its significance. My recent experience and my research have changed my view and my practice. To my great benefit, I have discovered and recovered the tremendous power of this most ancient Christian prayer.

Sometimes as I sign myself, I imagine that I have traveled back through time to Calvary. With Mary, Mary Magdalene, and John, I stand at the foot of the cross as a witness to the Lord's supreme sacrifice. I watch him die a horrific death out of love for me. Then a soldier pierces his side and a flood of graces flow from his heart, engulfing me in unimaginable blessings. With this book I encourage you to join me at his cross. Come with me to Golgotha where you also will discover the life-transforming power of the holy gesture and open yourself more fully to its wonderful graces.

I invite you to explore with me the multidimensional realities of the sign of the cross. If you accept—and I hope you do, for I know you will not regret it—we will discuss together the following six truths that will enhance your experience of the ancient prayer. The sign of the cross is

- an act of faith that brings us into God's presence,
- a way to renew our Baptism,
- an affirmation of our decision to follow Christ,
- a decision to accept our share in Christ's suffering,
- a defense against the devil, and
- a means to overcome our faults and to grow in likeness to Christ.

When Jim Manney, my friend and editor, heard me speak about these truths, he said that the sign of the cross summed up the entire Christian life and that he wanted me to write a book about it. I agreed with his assertion and his request. I wrote this book to present this most ancient Christian prayer gesture as a simple and reliable way for us to renew our Christian lives.

A Fount of Blessing

My enthusiasm for the sign of the cross, multiplied by the enthusiasm of the early writers whom I cite, may lead you to a false conclusion about how it works. Let's be clear up front that the gesture does not *cause* blessing or empowerment. Rather, the sign of the cross *opens* us to God's blessing and power. Distinguishing sacramentals from sacraments will help us get this right.

The Church calls the sign of the cross a *sacramental* because it operates like a *sacrament*. But a sacramental differs significantly from a sacrament. A sacrament is a sign or symbol that causes what it signifies. For example, in Baptism, God uses water, a symbol of cleansing, to wash away all of our sins. A sacramental does not confer divine graces the same way a sacrament does, but rather it prepares us to receive God's blessing and disposes us to cooperate with it. When we make the sign of the cross, for example, we open ourselves to the Lord's doing something in us. We are preparing ourselves for his blessing and expressing our desire to receive and use it. A sacrament causes; a sacramental invites.

Every time we make the sign of the cross, we invite the Lord to bless us, and he always responds. We may sense his action as Solzhenitsyn did when he recovered hope. But most often when we sign ourselves, we don't feel anything. That's because God is using the movements of our body to reach our spirit, and our senses cannot register much of what he does there. Yet each time we make the sign, the Lord gives us a new burst of divine energy. When we touch our forehead, breast, and shoulders in his name, he touches our spirit with the blessings of the cross.

The Church uses the word *grace* to describe the blessing bestowed on us through the sacraments and sacramentals. *Grace* refers to an outpouring of the Holy Spirit that comes to us as God's free gift. *Sanctifying grace* is the presence of the Spirit that saves us and makes us holy. *Actual grace* refers to a specific gift of divine energy that supports our Christian life. Solzhenitsyn, for example, abided in the sanctifying grace that flooded him at his Baptism, and the divine intervention that gave him hope to endure the gulag was an actual grace.

Like all sacramentals, the sign of the cross disposes us to make better use of sanctifying grace and calls on God to give us actual graces. The *Catechism of the Catholic Church* emphasizes this reality:

> For well-disposed members of the faithful, the liturgy of the sacraments and sacramentals sanctifies almost every event of their lives with the divine grace which flows from the Paschal mystery of the Passion, Death, and Resurrection of Christ. From this source all sacraments and sacramentals draw their power. There is scarcely

any proper use of things which cannot be thus directed toward the sanctification of men and the praise of God.[6]

Here the *Catechism* adopts and recommends the ancient Christian practice of consecrating daily life with sacramentals, the chief of which is the sign of the cross. Invoking the blessing of the sign at key moments elevates ordinary activities into opportunities for drawing nearer to God— activities such as waking up, eating, driving the children to school, starting your workday, responding to your email, shopping, relaxing with your family, and going to bed.

Blessing others and objects with the sign of the cross is also an ancient Christian practice. We make the sign in the air over a person or thing while invoking the name of the Father, the Son, and the Holy Spirit. The Church extensively employs this form of the sign of the cross as a blessing in the liturgy. During Mass, for example, the celebrant makes the sign over the bread and wine to prepare them for the sacrifice, and at the end of Mass, he signs a blessing over the people to strengthen them for their service of God and others. Outside the liturgy, priests bless religious objects like rosaries, medals, scapulars, or small crucifixes.

I find it difficult to apply the recommendations of many spiritual books. They overwhelm me with recipes of seven, twelve, or 144 things that I must do to achieve spiritual success, or with complex programs of spiritual disciplines that require more effort than I can muster. While I admire the wisdom of such books, I rarely am able to do what they suggest. You may feel the same way. But the advice I am giving in this little book requires only the effort of making a simple gesture and praying a simple prayer. Christ did the hard work when he endured his excruciating Passion and death and made his cross a fount of blessing for us. You can start right now to enjoy more fully the blessings and power of this ancient sign. Just trace it on your body with reverence and faith. Go ahead, do it—even if you are reading this in a public place.

Before we consider together the six truths that will broaden your understanding and experience of the sign of the cross, I want to tell you how Christians have made it in the past, and how we have come to make the large and little signs that we make today. But if you are not curious about the history of the ancient prayer, you may skip to chapter three and plunge into the core message of this book.

CHAPTER TWO
A Short History of the Sign of the Cross

"Go . . . all through Jerusalem and mark a cross on the foreheads of all who grieve and lament over the loathsome practices in it."

—EZEKIEL 9:4

And then ye bless you with the sygne of the holy crosse. . . . And in thys blessinge ye beginne with youre hande from the hedde downward, and then to the lefte side and after to the right side, in token and byleve that Our Lord Jesu Christe came down from the head, that is from the Father into the erthe by his holy Incarnation, and from the erthe into the left side, that is hell, by his bitter Passion, and from thence unto his Father's ryghte side by his glorious Ascension.[1]

—MYROURE OF OUR LADYE (fifteenth century)

As soon as you get out of bed in the morning, you should bless yourself with the sign of the holy cross and say: "May the will of God, the Father, the Son, and the Holy Spirit be done! Amen."[2]

—MARTIN LUTHER (1483–1546)

✠

During the Reformation of the sixteenth century, some Christians repudiated the sign of the cross because they judged it to be superstitious. But Martin Luther himself did not abandon it and recommended the practice in his *Small Catechism* in an appendix on family prayer. Today, athletes who sign themselves for good luck at sporting events reinforce the opinion that it is a superstition. But basketball players at the foul line were not the first to abuse the gesture by ascribing to it magical powers that could be turned to dubious personal advantage. As early as the sixth century, St. Caesarius (470–542), the bishop of Arles and one of Christianity's first best-selling authors, rebuked Christians who signed themselves while on their way to steal or commit adultery.[3]

But no trace of superstition or magic marred the sign of the cross in its origins. While no direct evidence exists, it seems clear from circumstances that the holy gesture had its roots as a prayer in apostolic times. Fourth-century Father of the Church St. Basil (329–379) said that the Apostles "taught us to mark with the sign of the cross those who put their hope in the Lord"[4]—that is, those who presented themselves for Baptism.

So early Christians probably learned to make the sign of the cross at their Baptism when the celebrant marked them with it to claim them for Christ. There is some evidence for this in Scripture. For example, St. Paul reminded the Ephesians that they received the sign at Baptism when he said: "You have been stamped with the seal of the Holy Spirit of the Promise" (1 Cor. 1:13). And Paul may have been speaking of his being signed with the cross at Baptism when he told the Galatians that "I carry branded on my body the marks of Jesus" (Gal. 6:17). I will say more about this later, but for now I merely want to show you that the sign of the cross originated among people who were not far removed from Christ himself.

Early Christians used the thumb or index finger to trace a little cross on their foreheads. They associated the practice with references in Ezekiel 9:7 and Revelation 7:3, 9:4, and 14:1, all of which describe believers bearing God's seal on their foreheads. That mark was a cross—the Greek letter *tau*—that was written as a **T** and stood for the name of God. Origen (c. 185–c. 253), a third-century theologian and spiritual writer, commented on the Ezekiel passage by quoting a writer who said:

> The shape of the letter tau presented a resemblance to the figure of the cross and this represented a prophecy of the sign that Christians make on their foreheads. For all the faithful make this sign when they undertake any activity, especially prayer or reading Holy Scripture.[5]

So by the third century, Christians frequently marked their foreheads with the cross. They also traced the little sign on their lips and breasts, as we still do today when the Gospel is announced at Mass. And they made the sign in the air as a blessing over persons and things. Tertullian, for example, told of a woman who signed her bed,[6] and St. Cyril of Jerusalem described Christians tracing the cross "over the bread we eat and the cups we drink."[7] Using the sign of the cross as a blessing may have prompted some Christians to make the larger sign that we know today, but that practice did not come into common use until later on.

Opposition to the Monophysite heresy in the seventh and eight centuries may have contributed to popularizing the larger sign. To summarily refute these heretics, who held that Christ had only one divine nature instead of two natures, one human and one divine, Christians in the East began to sign themselves with two fingers or with the thumb and forefinger. They had to trace a larger sign over their breasts so that their use of two fingers to defend the truth would be visible to all. Imagine the duel that occurred when a Christian encountered a Monophysite. The Christian would conspicuously make a large sign with two fingers and hurry to the other side of the street. The Monophysite would respond with a large sign made with his index finger and walk off in a huff. The idea of that scene may make us smile, but in those days ordinary folks' tempers flared over theological issues.

By the ninth century, Christians in the East were making the larger gesture with thumb and two fingers displayed, symbolizing the Trinity, and with the ring and little finger folded back, symbolizing Christ's two natures. In the middle of the eighth century, at a time when emperors had a lot to say about ecclesiastical matters, Byzantine emperor Leo IV decreed that all blessings should be made with a large right cross—that is, with the horizontal gesture moving from right to left. Although this proclamation applied to blessings, it was popularly adapted to the gesture of signing oneself. The emperor's directive established the large sign as the common practice in the East. Christians of the Eastern Churches signed themselves with two fingers and thumb extended, touching their forehead and moving to their breast, then crossing their shoulders from right to left.

How Western Christians came to adopt the larger sign of the cross is less clear. Apparently after the ninth century some Western Christians imitated the practice of the Eastern Church and signed themselves with a large right cross. But at the same time others in the West had begun to trace the large cross over their breasts moving their hand from the left shoulder to the right shoulder.

Innocent III (1160–1216), who was pope at the beginning of the thirteenth century, directed that Christians sign themselves with two fingers and thumb extended. He allowed that some make a right cross and others a left cross, indicating no preference for either approach. But before the end of the Middle Ages, Western Christians showed a preference for signing themselves with a large left cross. For example, the *Myroure of Our Ladye*, a late-fifteenth-century document, taught the Brigittine Sisters of Syon Abbey in Middlesex, England, to cross themselves from left to right. It explained that the movement from forehead to breast meant that Christ came down from heaven to earth in his Incarnation, and the movement from the left to right shoulder indicated that Christ at his death descended into hell and then ascended to heaven to sit at the Father's right hand.

By the end of the Middle Ages, probably under the extensive influence of Benedictine monasteries, where the practice was to make a large left cross with an open hand, most Western Christians were making the sign of the cross as we do today.

In every age Christians commonly, but not indispensably, accompanied the act of making the sign with words of prayer. But the prayers varied greatly. In the earlier period, they used invocations like "The sign of Christ," "The seal of the living God," and "In the name of Jesus." In later ages, they prayed, "In the name of Jesus of Nazareth," "In the name of the Holy Trinity," and "In the name of the Father, and of the Son, and of the Holy Spirit," the latter being the most common prayer that we use today. Christians have also used formulas suggested by the liturgy, like "O God come to my assistance" and "Our help is in the name of the Lord."[8] This diversity of words accompanying the sign should encourage you to pray spontaneously when you cross yourself, a practice that I recommend in later chapters.

Twenty-first-century Christians have inherited a diversity of ways to make the sign. Today you will see people marking themselves with large left crosses or large right crosses, with open hand or with two fingers and thumb extended; tracing little crosses on their foreheads, lips, and breasts with one finger, two fingers, or with thumb and forefinger. You may see a Latino youth make a large left cross and then kiss a little cross made with thumb and forefinger, a practice rooted in the ancient past. You will see clergy in liturgical settings and laypeople in ordinary situations blessing persons and objects with two fingers and a thumb or an open hand. But no matter how they do it, large or small, with one finger, two, three, or an open hand, all who sign themselves with faith are opening themselves to the Lord. We will begin to examine the ways that this sign opens us to God in the next chapter.

CHAPTER THREE
An Opening to God

Whatever you say or do, let it be in the name of the Lord Jesus, in thanksgiving to God the Father through him.

—COLOSSIANS 3:17

Whatever you ask in my name I will do, so that the Father may be glorified in the Son. If you ask me anything in my name, I will do it.

—JOHN 14:13–14

When you sign yourself, think of all the mysteries contained in the cross. It is not enough to form it with the finger. You must first make it with faith and good will. . . . When you mark your breast, your eyes, and all your members with the sign of the cross, offer yourself as a victim pleasing to God.[1]

—ST. JOHN CHRYSOSTOM (347–407)

If you decide to recover the benefits of the ancient Christian practice, you will sign yourself as frequently as the early Christians did. You will discover, as I promised in chapter one, that the sign releases a flow of blessings in your life. That's because the sign of the cross and the words we pray when making it open us to God. Here's how.

Sometimes we sign ourselves silently, opening to its blessing without saying any accompanying words. For example, I quietly mark myself when I board an airplane or walk through a busy intersection. But while making the sign, we often say, "In the name of the Father, and of the Son, and of the Holy Spirit. Amen." We call upon the Lord in this way especially when we begin or end our prayers. That's how the Christian community begins its celebration of our greatest prayer, the Mass. And the Mass always ends with the priest's cruciform blessing of the assembly.

Making the sign with the invocation of the Trinity renews our spiritual energy in several ways. It gives us an opportunity to

- profess our faith,
- pray to God as he is (not as we imagine him to be),

- enter into his presence, and
- pray with "Godpower" (as opposed to mere "humanpower").

Consider these realities with me. Reflecting on them will change the way you make the sign of the cross. And signing yourself more thoughtfully will open you more fully to God and strengthen your relationship with him. Few spiritual disciplines offer so much benefit for so little effort as this ancient and holy gesture.

Professing Our Faith

The prayer that we say while making the sign derives from Jesus' command, reported in Matthew 28:19, that the Church should baptize new disciples "in the name of the Father and of the Son and of the Holy Spirit." This formula evolved into longer creeds by which converts declared their faith at Baptism. By the end of the fourth century, newly baptized Christians in the churches of the East professed the Nicene Creed, which we now recite at Sunday Mass. Converts in Western churches confessed the Apostles' Creed, which an ancient legend claims that the Twelve collaborated to compose. The text of that familiar prayer reads as follows:

I believe in God,
the Father almighty,
creator of heaven and earth.
And in Jesus Christ, his only Son, our Lord,
who was conceived by the Holy Spirit,

born of the Virgin Mary,
suffered under Pontius Pilate,
> was crucified, died, and was buried;
> he descended into hell;
On the third day he rose again from the dead;
he ascended into heaven
> and is seated at the right hand of God the Father
> > almighty;
> from there he will come to judge the living and
> > the dead.
I believe in the Holy Spirit,
> the holy catholic Church,
> the communion of saints,
> the forgiveness of sins,
> the resurrection of the body,
> and life everlasting. Amen.[2]

Each time we make the sign of the cross, we renew our profession of faith in these truths in an abbreviated but spiritually dense form. We express our belief in, and commitment to, the Father, Son, and Holy Spirit, and we acknowledge their work of creation, salvation, and sanctification.

In the past, many Christians believed that even without our pronouncing the words, the gesture itself confessed our faith. They held that making the sign affirmed essential Christian doctrines: Touching our forehead and descending to our breast declared that we believe the Father sent his Son from heaven to earth to assume our human nature. Touching the left shoulder confessed that the Son died on the cross to bring us salvation. And moving to the right shoulder professed our faith in his Ascension to heaven and his sending of the Holy Spirit to sanctify us.

The sign of the cross holds us to these Christian realities. It assures our loyalty to God and our fidelity to basic Christian doctrines, and so contributes significantly to our spiritual well-being. We should do it deliberately and often.

Addressing God as He Is

Relying too heavily on our own idea of God may weaken or distort our relationship with him. But invoking the Trinity when we sign ourselves helps us avoid this unhappy condition. Here's how our imagination may cloud our relationship with God and how the sign of the cross keeps it clear.

Recently an interviewer on a national radio program asked listeners what they did when they prayed. One woman said she imagined God as being "very, very big" and herself as "very, very small" as she stood before him. Another person said he just "climbed up onto God's lap and sat there with him." Using our imagination like this can enhance our prayer, but it may also inhibit our coming to know God better and love him more.

In a worst-case scenario, too much imagining may even cause us to be worshiping our own idea of God instead of God himself. In C.S. Lewis' classic *The Screwtape Letters*, Screwtape, a senior devil who is training his nephew Wormwood to seduce souls, advises him to encourage his "patient" to pray to the mental picture of God (whom Screwtape calls the "Enemy") that he has constructed for himself. The humans, says Screwtape,

> do not start from that direct perception of Him which we, unhappily, cannot avoid. . . . If you look into your patient's mind when he is praying, you will not find *that*. If you examine the object to which he is attending, you will find that it is a composite object containing many quite ridiculous ingredients. There will be images derived from pictures of the Enemy as He appeared during the discreditable episode known as the Incarnation: there will be vaguer—perhaps quite savage and puerile—images associated with the other two Persons. . . . But whatever the nature of the composite object, you must keep him praying to *it*—to the thing that he has made, not to the Person who has made him. . . . For if he ever comes to make the distinction, if ever he consciously directs his prayers "Not to what I think thou art but to what thou knowest thyself to be," our situation is, for the moment, desperate. Once all his thoughts and images have been flung aside or, if retained, retained with a full recognition of their subjective nature, and the man trusts himself to the completely real, external, invisible Presence, there with him in the room and never knowable by him as he is known by it—why, then it is that the incalculable may occur.[3]

Here's where the sign of the cross comes in. When we invoke the Trinity, we fix our attention on the God

25

who made us, not the idea of God we have made. We are flinging our images aside and addressing our prayers to God as he has revealed himself: Father, Son, and Holy Spirit. Sometimes after I have signed myself with the Trinitarian formula, to be sure I'm getting it right I add: "Lord, I am praying to you as the God who knows who he is, not to one that I think I know." In so fixing my gaze on God as he is, I expect the incalculable to occur. I urge you to try it. You will soon notice a difference in your prayer and your disposition toward the Lord.

Coming into God's Presence

The meaning associated with the word *name* has thinned down over the centuries. It has lost considerable weight since its usage in the Bible where it conveyed a heavier meaning than it does now. If we are going to experience the full benefit of praying "In the *name* of the Father, and of the Son, and of the Holy Spirit," we must recover the rich connotation that Scripture applies to the name of God.

We regard a name as a label. It simply identifies the person who bears it. But for Jews in biblical times, a name did much more. It bore the person's nature and substance. Consider two examples, one from the Old Testament and another from the New Testament. When Jacob triumphed in his wrestling match with God, God gave him a new name that communicated his nature: "No longer are you to be called Jacob, but Israel since you have shown your strength against God and men and have prevailed" (Gen. 32:29). The name "Israel" means "he who strives with God."

And when Jesus met Simon, he immediately gave him a new name that expressed his substance: "'So you are Simon the son of John? You shall be called Cephas' (which means Peter)" (John 1:42 RSV). Both names mean "rock," *Cephas* in Aramaic and *Peter* in Greek.

Similarly, the name of God carries his nature and substance. When Moses asked God his name, he replied, "I am he who is." God also said to Moses, "This is what you are to say to the Israelites, 'I am has sent me to you'" (Exod. 3:14). The Jewish writers of Scripture wrote this name as YHWH, which we now pronounce as "Yahweh." Jesus spoke his divine name to Jewish leaders in a confrontation over his relationship to Abraham: "In all truth I tell you before Abraham ever was, *I am*" (John 8:58; emphasis added). So God has revealed to us his name, a name that sums up his infinite existence and communicates it to us.

This biblical understanding of God's name opens us more fully to the spiritual power of the sign of the cross. When we make it "in the name of" the Holy Trinity, we are praying in accord with God's divine nature and substance. We are praying in union with the God who is. Thus, the invocation transports our prayer to a higher level by bringing us into the Lord's presence and engaging his power. For Scripture teaches that when we call upon his name, God draws near and blesses us. For example, when God made his covenant with Israel, he promised, "Wherever I choose to have my name remembered, I shall come to you and bless you" (Exod. 20:24). He also instructed Moses to have the priests bless the Israelites by calling upon his name—Yah-weh, "I am he who is":

> Yahweh spoke to Moses and said, "Speak to Aaron
> and his sons and say: 'This is how you must bless the
> Israelites. You will say:
>> May Yahweh bless you and keep you.
>> May Yahweh let his face shine on you, and be
>>> gracious to you.
>> May Yahweh show you his face and bring you
>>> peace.'
> This is how they must call down my name on the Israel-
> ites, and then I shall bless them." (Num. 6:22–27)

With the sign of the cross we remember God's name, and in response he takes us into his presence and blesses us. So it is not merely a formula that opens and closes our prayers. The sign is an action that draws us near to God and makes us aware that we walk and pray in his company. Such a little gesture, so wonderful a consequence.

Praying with Godpower

Invoking God's name supernaturalizes our natural prayer. I like to say that by signing myself I am praying with Godpower instead of with humanpower, and praying with Godpower makes a world of difference. By praying in God's name, I am lining up my nature and substance with his nature and substance. This is what Jesus meant when he taught that if we asked anything in his name he would grant it. He repeated this promise five times in his farewell to the disciples the night before he died. He wanted to impress upon us the tremendous advantage we have in calling upon his name. Jesus was also aware of our thick-headedness and used repetition to break through it. Just let his words sink into your mind and heart:

> John 14:13–14: "Whatever you ask in my name I will do, so that the Father may be glorified in the Son. If you ask me anything in my name, I will do it."

> John 15:16: "The Father will give you anything you ask him in my name."

> John 16:23: "In all truth I tell you, anything you ask of the Father he will grant in my name.

> John 16:26–27: "When that day comes you will ask in my name; and I do not say that I shall pray to the Father for you, because the Father himself loves you for loving me, and believing that I came from God."

Jesus does not mean that we can get whatever we want by tacking the formula "in Jesus' name" onto our prayer requests. Rather, he teaches us to align our wills to God's will so that we will want what he wants and our prayer will become his prayer. That's the thrust of the prayer that the Lord gave us: "Our Father who art in heaven, / Hallowed be thy name. / Thy kingdom come, / Thy will be done, / On earth as it is in heaven" (Matt. 6:9–10 RSV). We reprise these words of the Lord's Prayer each time we sign ourselves.

The sign of the cross, then, with its lovely gesture and words, declares our decision to remain one with God and to embrace his will as our own. So praying *in the name of* the Blessed Trinity assures us that the Lord will answer our prayers because we will be learning how to pray for what he has foremost in his heart.

After I discovered the truths I have laid out in this chapter, I could never again make the sign of the cross casually. I make it with reverence and deliberation as an act of faith; as an appeal to God as he is, not as I imagine him; and as a calling upon his name that takes me into his presence and aligns my will with his. I hope these truths touch you in the same way.

CHAPTER FOUR
A Renewal of Baptism

You cannot have forgotten that all of us, when we were baptized into Christ Jesus, were baptized into his death. So by our baptism into his death we were buried with him, so that as Christ was raised from the dead by the Father's glorious power, we too should begin living a new life.

—ROMANS 6:3–4

We come to the font as to the Red Sea. Moses was the leader in saving Israel; Christ was the leader in redeeming the human race. . . . The vast sea is divided by a rod; the entrance to the font is opened with the sign of the cross. Israel enters the sea; man is washed in the font.[1]

—ST. ILDEFONSUS OF TOLEDO (c. 607–667)

Let us not be ashamed of the Cross of Christ, but even if someone else conceals it, you must carry its mark publicly on your forehead, so that the demons, seeing the royal sign, trembling, may fly far away. Make this sign when you eat and when you drink, when you sit down, when you go to bed, when you get up, when you speak—in a word, on all occasions.[2]

—ST. CYRIL OF JERUSALEM (c. 315–386)

✝

Every year on a Sunday in Lent millions of Catholics witness a striking reenactment of an ancient Christian ceremony. During Mass on that day, women and men who will be baptized at Easter are presented to the congregation. Their sponsors stand before them and claim them for Christ with the sign of the cross. The rite does not stop with the first little mark that the sponsor traces on his candidate's forehead. He then multiplies the sacred gesture, signing the candidate's eyes, ears, mouth, shoulders, hands, and feet. Finally, in a magnificent climax, he makes the sign of the cross over the person's entire body. This dramatic event thrills me each time I see it. I feel as though I have been transported back in time to a gathering in first-century Jerusalem and am watching the original Christian community prepare candidates for Baptism.

As we have seen, receiving the mark of Christ at Baptism taught the early Christians to make the sign of the cross (see pp. 14-15). And they kept in mind the connection between their baptismal signing and their signing themselves as a way of releasing the sacrament's power in their lives. St. Cyril of Jerusalem, for example, instructed new

Christians both to bear confidently the baptismal mark in their persons and to sign themselves in all circumstances:

> Let us not be ashamed of the cross of Christ, but even if someone else conceals it, *you must carry its mark publicly on your forehead*, so that the demons, seeing the royal sign, trembling, may fly far away. *Make this sign* when you eat and when you drink, when you sit down, when you go to bed, when you get up, when you speak—in a word, on all occasions.[3]

We will do well to imitate our ancestors by making the same connection between our Baptism and the sign of the cross. For making the sign with faith activates the spiritual power of our Baptism. Let's talk about it.

Three truths help me realize how signing myself awakens me to the spiritual energy that God gave me at my Baptism. I share them with you here so that you may also experience more fully the blessing and power of the cross. The sign of the cross reminds me of the following realities and opens me to their graces. In my Baptism:

- I joined Christ in his death and rose with him to a new, supernatural life.
- Christ, by his cross, freed me from slavery to sin and death.
- The Lord marked me with the sign of the cross as the seal of my participation in the New Covenant and my incorporation into the Body of Christ.

Think about these things with me and see how making the sign of the cross empowers us for daily Christian living.

A Sign of Supernatural Life

Immersion in water or pouring water is the matter of the sacramental sign of Baptism. The symbol speaks to us of water's cleansing power, and our first thought about it is that God uses it in Baptism to wash away our sins. That's what the Church has always taught.[4] But the first thought of early Christians about the symbol was not water's power to cleanse but its power to kill. For the Fathers of the Church, our immersion in water at Baptism was a death—our participation in the death and rising of Christ.

St. Paul was the first to develop this teaching, and he expressed it most directly in his letter to the Romans. "When we were baptized into Christ Jesus," he said, "we were baptized into his death. So by our Baptism into his death we were buried with him, so that as Christ was raised from the dead by the Father's glorious power, we too should begin living a new life" (Rom. 6:3–4). The Fathers elaborated on this theme, paralleling the actions of the sacrament to the events of the Crucifixion. St. Cyril of Jerusalem, for example, explained Baptism to new Christians in this way:

> Then you were led to the holy pool of divine Baptism, as Christ was carried from the cross to the tomb. . . . And each of you was asked whether he believed in the name of the Father, and of the Son, and of the Holy Spirit. You made that saving confession and you descended three times into the water and ascended, symbolizing the three days of Christ's burial. . . . For by this immersion and rising you were both dying and being born.

That water of salvation was at once your grave and your mother.[5]

We must bring this truth to bear on our understanding of the way that Baptism frees us of original sin. We tend to think of original sin as a stain on our souls inherited from Adam that the water of Baptism washes away. But St. Paul and the Fathers of the Church thought about it differently. They saw the consequence of Adam's disobedience not as a disfiguring of his soul but as the tragic loss of the supernatural life that God had given him and planned to give to the whole human race. At the tree of the knowledge of good and evil, Adam forfeited the benefits bestowed on him by God, especially the grace of sharing in the divine life. Consequently, we must understand original sin as a great deprivation. But by his obedience at the tree of the cross, Jesus recovered for us supernatural life with all of its benefits, including the capacity to see God face-to-face, which will be our reward in heaven. And by our dying and rising with him in our Baptism, we receive the gift of that supernatural life that Adam had originally lost. "Just as all die in Adam," said St. Paul, "so in Christ all will be brought to life" (1 Cor. 15:22).

As God does in all sacraments, he allows the sign of Baptism to accomplish what it signifies. He lets water cause our participation in Christ's death and rising. While making the sign of the cross reminds us of our Baptism, the gesture itself does not possess any sacramental power. But tracing the cross on our bodies and repeating the formula of Baptism ("In the name of the Father . . .") expresses our faith and opens us to all the benefits of the new life Christ won for us.

A Sign of Our Spiritual Freedom

Early Christian writers regarded God's delivering Israel from slavery in Egypt at the Red Sea as a foreshadowing of his delivering us from slavery to sin and death at our Baptism. They saw Moses' rod as a type of Christ's cross. "We come to the font as to the Red Sea," said Ildefonsus of Toledo, one of Spain's most loved saints. He continued:

> The Egyptians pursued the Israelites; sin pursued us. The sea is colored by the red of its shore; baptism is consecrated with the blood of Christ. The vast sea is divided by a rod; the entrance to the font is opened with the sign of the cross. Israel enters the sea; we are washed in the font. . . . The pursuing Egyptians are drowned with Pharaoh; sins are destroyed in baptism together with the devil in a destruction not of life but of power.[6]

We believe that Baptism frees us from sin and death, and making the sign of the cross can play a very practical role in applying this truth to our lives. Signing ourselves can help us experience our spiritual freedom. Let's see what it can do to keep us free of sin and its consequences.

In Romans 6, Paul suggests that it is not enough to realize that by Baptism we are dead to sin. Listen to what he says:

> We *know* that our old self was crucified with him so that the sinful body might be destroyed, and we might no

longer be enslaved to sin. . . . So you also must *consider* yourselves dead to sin and alive to God in Christ Jesus. Let not sin therefore reign in your mortal bodies to make you obey their passions. *Do not yield* your members to sin as instruments of wickedness, but *yield yourselves to God* as men who have been brought from death to life, and your members to God as instruments of righteousness (Rom. 6:6, 11–13 RSV; emphasis added).

We may *know* that we have died to sin, but if we fail to act on that knowledge, we may still give in to it. Paul insists that we must hold ourselves to the truth—we must "consider ourselves dead to sin and alive to God." That means we must think about it, regard it, dwell on it, mull over it, meditate on it, ponder it, take it into account, and so on.

He also insists that we must refuse to yield to sin and that we must decide to yield ourselves to God. That means we must not give in, give way, surrender, or submit to sin, but must give in, give way, surrender, and submit to God.

That's what we do when we make the sign of the cross. Signing ourselves is a way of considering ourselves dead to sin and alive to God. It is a practical means for refusing to yield to sin and for yielding ourselves to God. So when temptation knocks, the sign of the cross is the best way to let it know that "no one's home." As St. Paul says, "Someone who has died, of course, no longer has to answer for sin" (Rom. 6:7).

A Sign of Membership in the Church

Scripture draws a parallel between circumcision and Baptism. St. Paul, for example, spoke about Baptism in this way: "In [Christ] you have been circumcised, with a circumcision performed, not by human hand, but by the complete stripping of your natural self. This is circumcision according to Christ" (Col. 1:11). Just as the rite of circumcision sealed the Old Testament alliance of God with his people and incorporated them into Israel, Baptism seals the New Covenant alliance of God with us and incorporates us into the new Israel, the Church. And just as circumcision marked the body as a sign of participation in the Old Covenant, Baptism marks us with a sign of our participation in the New Covenant—the sign of the cross.

At Baptism, the celebrant, sponsor, and parents (if the candidate is an infant) seal our union with God and membership in the Body of Christ by marking our bodies with the sign of the cross. God seals our spirits to mark these relationships. Again speaking of Baptism, St. Paul says, "You have been stamped with the seal of the Holy Spirit" (Eph. 1:13). And Baptism is the doorway to our celebrating all of the other sacraments because until we are sealed by the Holy Spirit, we do not have access to their spiritual benefits. When we trace the cross over our bodies, we acknowledge what Baptism has accomplished for us. It announces our participation in the New Covenant and our membership in the Church.

The early Christians traced the cross on their foreheads to remind themselves that by Baptism they lived a supernatural life in the Body of Christ. The external mark expressed an inner grace, the presence of God himself. It works the same for us today. Each time we trace the cross over our breasts, we renew our Baptism, asking the Lord to refresh our life in the Holy Spirit. I recommend that you do this deliberately. Sign yourself, and as you pray the words that consecrated you to the Lord in Baptism, ask him to strengthen your union with him and to energize you with a new outpouring of the Holy Spirit. Can you think of an easier way to bring the grace of the sacrament to your life? Can you imagine any simpler way to fully employ the spiritual power the Lord has placed at your disposal? I can't. As we trace the sign of the cross over our body, we should recall the stream of grace that flowed into us in Baptism.

A simple gesture that we always perform sums up the truths of this chapter. Each time we enter a church before Mass, we dip our fingers into holy water and make the sign of the cross. We must recognize the significance of that action. For by that sign we are reminding ourselves that we have been baptized; that we have died with Christ and risen to a new life with him; that the cross has freed us from sin and death; that we are members of the Body of Christ; and that marked by the sign of the cross we are authorized to participate in the Holy Eucharist, the highest of the sacraments, and to offer with the Lord his perfect sacrifice.

Jesus designed Baptism as a source of new life for those he called to become his disciples, and in the next chapter we consider the connection between the sign of the cross and following him. You will notice that from this point on the going gets tougher. Making the sign calls for follow-through actions that require hard decisions. Its demands are difficult, but it offers great spiritual rewards.

CHAPTER FIVE
A Mark of Discipleship

Then he said to them all: "Whoever wants to be my disciple must deny themselves and take up their cross daily and follow me."

—LUKE 9:23 (NIV)

As soon as the Redeemer had restored us to our liberty he marked us with his sign, the sign of the cross. So we bear on our forehead the same sign that is engraved on the doors of palaces. The Conqueror places it there so that all may know that he has reentered into possession of us, and that we are his palaces, his living temples.[1]

—ST. CAESARIUS OF ARLES (470–542)

Thanks be to thee, my Lord Jesus Christ, for all the benefits thou hast given me, for all the pains and insults thou hast borne for me. O most merciful redeemer, friend and brother, may I know thee more clearly, love thee more dearly, and follow thee more nearly, day by day.[2]

—ST. RICHARD DE WYCHE (1197–1253)

✠

aking the sign of the cross declares publicly that I am a Christian. I am saying to all that I am a follower of Christ. That's a serious matter, given what Christ requires of all his disciples. "Whoever wants to be my disciple," he said, "must deny themselves and take up their cross daily and follow me. For whoever wants to save their life will lose it, but whoever loses their life for me will save it" (Luke 9:23–24 NIV).

If we think we are following a meek and mild Jesus who will make things easy for us, we had better think again. We follow him at a great cost, but he rewards us with greater benefits. Evangelical missionary Oswald Chambers (1874–1917) said that the Lord calls us to give our "utmost for his highest." That's what we are promising when we sign ourselves. So we dare not do it casually or carelessly.

Signaling Our Self-Denial

Jesus said that his followers must deny themselves. We usually understand this obligation to mean that the Lord requires us to undertake the kind of fasting that we practice during Lent. In that season, we abstain from meat, give up candy or desserts, skip meals, and so on. Jesus surely had such fasting in mind when he called us to deny ourselves. He predicted that his followers would fast when he was gone and prescribed that we do our fasting secretly (see Matt. 6:16–18; 9:15). He taught us to renounce our selfish attachments to the good things of earth as a way to anticipate the better things of heaven.

But when Jesus said that his followers must deny themselves, he also meant something else. Something deeper. He was establishing the terms on which he would relate to us, he as master and we as his disciples. As the condition of accepting us as followers, Jesus requires us to surrender control of our lives to him. Here Jesus, our Lord and teacher, was following the practice of the Jewish rabbis of his day who demanded the total submission of their pupils. This is the true meaning of self-denial: Jesus expects us to *deny* that we belong to ourselves and to *declare* that we belong to him.

The Fathers of the Church taught that this shift in ownership occurred at our Baptism when the celebrant marked us with the sign of the cross. They used the Greek word *sphragis* to name both the baptismal seal and the sign of the cross, a term that was pregnant with meaning about discipleship.

In the ancient world, a *sphragis* was a sign of ownership that a person placed on his possessions. For example, a shepherd marked his sheep as his property with a brand that he called a *sphragis*. And Roman generals claimed new recruits by tattooing a *sphragis* on their forearms, usually an abbreviated form of his name. The *sphragis* was not only a declaration of ownership. It also brought benefits to those that it marked. A shepherd protected and provided for those sheep that carried his brand. The general pledged loyalty and support to the soldiers who wore his sign.

The Fathers of the Church borrowed from the ancient practice of branding sheep and soldiers to explain how Christ claimed us as his own in Baptism. They taught that Christ used the sign of the cross to incorporate new believers into his flock. For instance, St. Cyril of Jerusalem, addressing candidates for Baptism, invited them to "come, receive the sacramental seal so that you may be easily recognized by the Master. Be numbered among the holy and spiritual flock of Christ, so that you may be set at his right hand and inherit the life prepared for you."[3]

The Fathers also taught that just as the shepherd's brand protected his sheep from danger, the sign of the cross defends us from our spiritual enemies. "If you fortify yourself with the sphragis," said St. Gregory Nazianzen (c. 329–390), "and secure yourself for the future with the best and strongest of all aids, being signed both in body and in soul with the anointing . . . what then can happen to you and what has been worked out for you? . . . This, even while you live, will greatly contribute to your sense of safety. For a sheep that is sealed is not easily snared, but that which is unmarked is an easy prey to thieves."[4]

For the Fathers, the general's marking soldiers with his name was even more helpful in explaining how Christ takes possession of us with the sign of the cross. When recruits enlisted in the Roman army, they participated in a religious ceremony during which they took a loyalty oath, called a *sacramentum*. Then, a general marked them as belonging to him with his *sphragis*. The Fathers saw a parallel between this practice and Baptism. At the beginning of Lent, the Church enlisted new believers in a formal ceremony in which they signed a registry that enrolled them for Baptism at Easter. At the Easter Vigil, the candidates declared their loyalty oath to Christ by professing faith in him. (The Fathers had in mind this Christian *sacramentum* when they invented the name for the Catholic sacraments). Then, through the agency of the celebrant, Christ marked their bodies and souls as belonging to him with his *sphragis*, the sign of the cross, which is the baptismal seal. St. Cyril put these words in the Lord's mouth: "After my battle on the cross, I gave to each of my soldiers the right to wear on their forehead the royal *sphragis*."[5]

So the sign of the cross says a lot about my relationship with the Lord. Making the cross over my body declares that

- I am his disciple;
- I no longer belong to myself, but I belong to him;
- I have been incorporated into his flock, bearing in my person the mark of his ownership;
- I have enlisted as a soldier in his army, proudly wearing his name on my forehead; and
- I count on him for his loyalty and protection.

Acknowledging the Lord's Ownership

It would be nice if we behaved as though we really believed that the Lord owned us. But we don't. We easily forget that we have entrusted ourselves to him and often conduct ourselves as though everything really belonged to us.

We must overcome the conditioning that trains us to believe that we own everything. We learn to say the words "my" and "mine" as toddlers, and then we apply them universally, from "my blanket" and "my puppy" to "my body, my time, and my life" and even to "my God." But a little clear thinking corrects our false perspectives.

We may forgive a toddler for believing that he owns the blanket that his mother knitted for him and the terrier that his father bought him. But we should rid ourselves of the notion that we own the bodies, time, and life that God gives us. Think about it. We arrive in a body and leave it at moments that God chooses without our consent. We have no control over time or life, which are God's constant gifts to us. "Who of you by worrying," asked Jesus, "can add a single hour to your life?" (Luke 12:25 NIV). And we make a horrific mistake if we reverse the true order of reality and dare to act as though the expression "my God" means something like "my puppy" instead of "the God that I worship."[6]

The sign of the cross helps us here. Making it frequently reminds us to recognize that we are the Lord's possession. It prompts us to behave as though we believed it. I sometimes sign myself, saying, "Lord, I acknowledge that you own me and everything about me." Then I sign myself again, saying, "Lord, I know that my body, my time, and my life really belong to you, not to me." And a third time, saying, "Lord, you are my God, the God that I worship with everything I have and am." I recommend this practice. I encourage you to make the sign of the cross while acknowledging in your own words that the Lord owns your body, time, and life—that he owns you.

Making this shift in ownership may at first strike you as burdensome and painful. None of us feels good about surrendering control over our time, our bodies, and our lives. But you will soon discover that acknowledging Christ's ownership relieves you of your burdens and pain. Entrusting yourself to the Lord alleviates your worry and allows you to receive his care. Jesus promised just that when he said, "Shoulder my yoke and learn from me, for I am gentle and humble in heart, *and you will find rest for your souls.* Yes, my yoke is easy and my burden light" (Matt. 11:29–30; emphasis added).

Following Jesus

Self-denial is the Lord's first condition for would-be disciples. He requires two things further. Disciples must take up their cross daily. Then they must follow him. We will consider the subject of bearing our crosses in the next chapter. Here let's talk about the role that the sign of the cross plays in our following of Jesus.

A disciple follows Jesus by embracing his teaching and obeying his commandments. Making the sign of the cross says that we accept these requirements of our discipleship. That's a big commitment, and to keep it we must understand all that it involves.

Embracing Christ's Teaching

This little book's limited scope prevents me from summarizing the Lord's teaching. But I can point readers in the right direction. We find Christ's teaching in the Bible, in the doctrine of the Church, and in books of theology. The place to start is the Gospels, especially with Jesus' longer discourses: the Sermon on the Mount (Matt. 5–7) and his farewell address (John 13:31–17:26). Then you will want to explore his instruction in the other New Testament books and the rest of the Bible.

The Lord made the Church the custodian of his teaching, and you will discover the heart of it in the *Catechism of the Catholic Church* and in the documents of the Second Vatican Council.[7] Among many excellent popular theology books that recap Christ's doctrine and reflect on it, I recommend my two favorites: *Theology and Sanity* by F.J. Sheed and *The Catholic Vision* by Edward D. O'Connor, CSC.[8]

We study Christ's teaching not to get better informed but to receive the truth and apply it to our lives. So as we read Scripture, the *Catechism*, and theology, we must ask questions such as "What is the Lord saying to me here?"; "What does this mean for me?"; and "What must I do about it?" It's just good common sense to begin our study by making the sign of the cross so that we approach the Lord's teaching by calling on his name.

Signing ourselves in the name of the Father, and of the Son, and of the Holy Spirit declares our desire to know all the truth that God has revealed about creation, redemption, and the spiritual life. Without these divinely inspired perspectives, said F.J. Sheed, we are doomed to a narrow-minded, insane view of things.[9] If we do not apprehend the truths the Lord has revealed, most of which are spiritual, invisible, and inaccessible to the senses, we are technically mad because we are out of touch with the greater part of reality. So I advise disciples to make the sign of the cross as an appeal to the Lord for his wisdom and for the mental and spiritual health that come from seeing things with his eyes.

Obeying Christ's Commandments

When we read the Gospels, we learn that Jesus not only affirmed the Ten Commandments but raised them to an even higher standard of holiness. "Do not imagine," he said, "that I have come to abolish the Law or the Prophets. I have come not to abolish but to complete them" (Matt. 5:17). He taught us that two great commandments sum up the Ten: "Love the Lord your God with all your heart and with all your soul and with all your mind" and "Love your neighbor as yourself" (Matt. 22:37, 39 NIV). He also gave us numerous specific commands such as "love your enemies" (Matt. 5:44), "do not store up for yourselves treasures on earth" (Matt. 6:19), and "do not judge" (Matt. 7:1).

We must not skip over any of these, but as good disciples we must determine how well we are obeying each of them. I find it helpful to ask myself the following question: What one thing can I do to obey more fully this command of Christ? When we are trying to figure out how to respond to a commandment, signing ourselves can help because it reminds us that Christ's own obedience took him to the cross. It signals our willingness to crucify our comfort, our preferences, our stubbornness, or anything that stands in the way of obeying him.

Just before he died, Jesus gave us the commandment to "love one another, as I have loved you. No one can have greater love than to lay down his life for his friends" (John 15:12–13). St. John explained the centrality of obeying Jesus' command in his first letter: "Whoever does not love does not know God, because God is love. . . . If we love one another, God lives in us and his love is made complete in us. . . . Whoever does not love their brother and sister, whom they have seen, cannot love God, whom they have not seen" (1 John 4:8, 12, 20 NIV). I believe that making the sign of the cross expresses our decision to obey this commandment of our Lord. I trace the vertical trunk of the cross from my head to my breast to pledge my love for God, and the horizontal bar across my shoulders to pledge my love for others. The act says that I lay down my life for others as a sign of my love for God.

CHAPTER SIX
An Acceptance of Suffering

"In the world you will have hardship, but be courageous: I have conquered the world."

—JOHN 16:33

Be merciful to me, O God, be merciful to me,
for in you my soul takes refuge;
in the shadow of your wings I will take refuge,
until the destroying storms pass by.

—PSALM 57:1 (NRSV)

In [Christ's] suffering he stretched forth his hands and measured out the world, that even then he might show that a great multitude, collected together out of all languages and tribes, from the rising of the sun even to its setting, was about to come under his wings, and to receive on their foreheads that great and lofty sign.[1]

—LACTANTIUS (c. 240–c. 320)

✛

We are tempted to believe that just by being good Christians, we can make suffering go away. We imagine that God's promise of blessing means that he will spare us all pain. But it doesn't work that way. Jesus made suffering a normal part of the Christian life. He promised his disciples multiple blessings, but tucked right in the middle of the good things that he said they could expect, he also promised suffering: "There is no one who has left house, brothers, sisters, mother, father, children or land for my sake and for the sake of the gospel who will not receive a hundred times as much houses, brothers, sisters, mothers, children and land—*and persecutions too*—now in the present time and, in the world to come, eternal life" (Mark 10:29–30; emphasis added). So suffering is not an option for Christians. It's a guarantee.

At its root, the word *suffering* means enduring pain or distress, sustaining loss or damage, being subject to disability or handicap, and ultimately submitting to death. It comes in all shapes. Daily nuisances frustrate us. Repeated failures discourage us. Bills we cannot pay pressure us. A disintegrating relationship racks us. Depression defeats us. Violence wounds us or a loved one. Illness ravages us or a family member. Suffering afflicts everybody—one size fits all.

Jesus did not only promise suffering, he made embracing it daily a requirement for all of his followers: "Then he said to them all: 'Whoever wants to be my disciple must deny themselves and take up their cross daily and follow me'" (Luke 9:23 NIV). Making the sign of the cross proclaims our yes to this condition of discipleship. When we sign ourselves, we are "taking up our cross" and accepting whatever suffering comes to us. With that ancient gesture, we are saying that we welcome our suffering on God's terms. Though we would rather not endure pain, we are subordinating our wills to God, just as Jesus subordinated his will to his Father when he gave himself to the cross. So tracing Christ's cross over our bodies is a serious matter. We must never do it casually.

Safety in the Shadow of His Wings

Christians attempt to comfort sufferers by touting the benefits of suffering. "Suffering builds character," we say. "I don't want character," says the sufferer, "I want relief." Then comes the inevitable question: "Where is God when it hurts?"

The mystery of the cross contains the answer. And signing ourselves opens us to hearing it. Let me explain this with a story.

At age twenty-three, Abby felt that her life was ruined. For three of her early teen years, an uncle had sexually abused her. Now anger and depression dominated her. She had to struggle to get through a day and cried herself to sleep at night. She had tried therapy and medications, but nothing helped. One day a friend urged Abby to consult Fr. Dan, a priest widely respected as a spiritual director. After a few "getting-to-know-you" visits, she trusted the priest enough to confide her terrible secret. "Where was God," she asked, "when my uncle was abusing me?"

"Why don't you ask God?" said Fr. Dan. Then he invited Abby to take some time to pray quietly in his chapel and remember a time when her uncle was forcing himself on her. Fr. Dan instructed Abby to put her question to the Lord and listen for his answer. Half an hour later Abby came from the chapel, weeping. "Well," asked Fr. Dan, "what happened? Did God answer your question?"

"Yes," said Abby. She smiled through her tears. "In my mind's eye I saw Jesus in the room with me while my uncle was hurting me. Jesus was weeping. He was with me all the time."

God comes to stay with us when we suffer. He shares our pain, sustains us, and comforts us. That's the message of the cross: God's only Son became a man in Christ. In his human nature, God himself suffered rejection, humiliation, ridicule, abandonment, buffetings, scourging, crucifixion, and death. He embraced suffering so that he could console us in our suffering.

Making the sign of the cross invites the Lord to join us in our suffering. We touch our forehead and move down to our breast, telling the Lord with this gesture that we want him to bend down to us. Then we cross our shoulders in a movement that asks him to support us—to shoulder us—in our suffering. Like the Psalmist who sought safety beneath the shadow of the Lord's wings, we sign ourselves, seeking safety beneath the shadow of his arms extended on the cross (see Psalms 17:8; 36:7; 57:1; 61:4; 63:7). The Lord's outstretched arms pledge that he understands our suffering and shares it with us.

Just as the Psalms anticipated the grace of Christ's Crucifixion, the Old Testament book of Deuteronomy provided another foreshadowing of the cross as a place of refuge. In Moses' farewell address, he seems to describe the silhouette of the cross in the far distance. He assured Israel that the arms of the Lord would uphold them through all their troubles: "The eternal God is your dwelling place, and underneath are the everlasting arms" (Deut. 33:27 RSV). Now we clearly see the cross as the sign that his everlasting arms uphold us through our troubles.

Sharing Christ's Suffering

In his Letter to the Colossians, St. Paul claims that we get to make up in our bodies what is lacking in the suffering of Christ. What could possibly be lacking, we ask, in the Lord's supreme sacrifice? On the cross he made a perfect offering that redeemed us from sin and reunited us to God. "It is finished" were Jesus' last words before he died (John 19:30).

But after Jesus had completed his great mission, he still had unfinished business with us. Paul says that Christ had to endure more suffering for his Church: "It makes me happy," he said, "to be suffering for you now, and in my own body to make up all the hardships that still have to be undergone by Christ for the sake of his body, the Church" (Col. 1:24). The "Christ" that Paul speaks about here is not merely the Jesus of the first century but Christ as he is now—the corporate Christ, the Body of Christ, the Church. Christ with the Body that he heads must continue to endure hardship, and as members of his Body, we have the privilege of joining him in his suffering. In this sense we get to make up in our bodies what was lacking in the suffering of Christ.

We face adversities every day because we are engaged with Christ in his spiritual combat for the Church. We easily lose sight of this reality and view our troubles and tragedies as inconveniences, bad luck, calamitous accidents, or "just the way things are." But from the beginning, Jesus conscripted his followers to join him in waging war against enemy forces that resist his effort to bring men and women into his kingdom. As St. Paul tells us, "You have been granted the privilege for Christ's sake not only of believing in him but of suffering for him as well; you are fighting the same battle which you saw me fighting for him and which you hear I am fighting still" (Phil. 1:29–30).

Our patient endurance of hardship in itself can contribute to Christ's work for the Church. It can become a prayer that touches the lives of others. Elisabeth Leseur (1866–1914), a candidate for canonization who suffered from cancer, taught that our suffering can become an opportunity of grace for others:

> I know all that suffering means, the fine and mysterious power it possesses, what it obtains and what it accomplishes. After all, our activity is of little importance. When Providence prefers to work by means of suffering, we should not complain. Then we can be sure that the work will be well done and not mixed up with all the misery of egotism and pride that sometimes spoil so much of our outward activity. I know by experience that in hours of trial certain graces are obtained for others that all our efforts had not previously obtained. I have thus concluded that suffering is the higher form of action, the best expression in the wonderful communion of saints. In suffering we are sure not to make mistakes, sure to be useful to others and to the great causes we long to serve.
>
> The Stoics said, "Suffering is nothing." They were wrong. Illuminated by a clearer light we Christians say, "Suffering is everything!" It demands, it obtains, everything. Through it God consents to accomplish everything. Suffering helps Christ to save the world and souls. When I am overwhelmed by the immensity of my desires for those I love, . . . it is toward suffering that I turn. It is through suffering that I ask to be allowed to serve as an intermediary between God and souls. It is the perfect form of prayer, the only infallible form of action. . . . Through the cross to the Light.[2]

After Elisabeth's death in 1914, her husband, Felix, who was an atheist, read her journals. He discovered there that she had offered years of great suffering for him. Felix was so moved that he not only embraced Christ but also became a Dominican priest, traveling throughout Europe speaking about his wife's spiritual writings.

A right and healthy perspective on suffering comes down to this: Christ won the war for our salvation on the cross, but he has engaged us to apply his victory in our daily lives. He has enlisted us as collaborators in his effort to draw people into his Church and defend it, and our collaboration with him opens us to suffering. As St. Ambrose once said— explaining why the wicked prosper—Trouble comes only to those on their way to glory. Making the sign of the cross over our bodies says yes both to the battle and to accepting hardship as our share in Christ's suffering.

CHAPTER SEVEN
A Defense Against the Devil

*This was the purpose of the appearing of the Son of God, to undo
the work of the devil.*

—1 JOHN 3:8

*Let us boldly make the sign of the cross on our foreheads with
our fingers, and over everything that we do: over the bread we
eat, and the cups we drink . . . when we lie down and when we
rise up. . . . It is a great protection—without price for the poor,
without toil for the sick—since also its grace is from God. It is
the sign of the faithful and the dread of devils, for . . . when they
see the cross, they are reminded of the Crucified; they are afraid
of him.*[1]

—ST. CYRIL OF JERUSALEM (c. 315–386)

*The sign of the cross is the type of our deliverance, the monument
of the liberation of mankind, the souvenir of the forbearance of
the Lord. When you make it, remember what has been given for
your ransom, and you will be the slave of no one. Make it, then
not only with your fingers, but with your faith. So if you engrave
it on your forehead, no impure spirit will dare to stand before
you. He sees the blade by which he has been wounded, the sword
by which he has received his death blow.*[2]

—ST. JOHN CHRYSOSTOM (347–407)

✠

When I give a talk about saints, someone invariably asks me why the Church demoted St. Christopher. I explain that the Church did not demote St. Christopher, but rather removed his feast day from the calendar of the saints because we have so little information about him. We know only that he died as a martyr during a persecution in the mid-third century.

Today, we revere and invoke St. Christopher as the patron of travelers, but we would do better to remember him for the reason he became a most popular saint in the Middle Ages. In those centuries, Christians celebrated him not because he guaranteed safety on the road or sea but because his legend demonstrated the power of the sign of the cross over the devil. Christopher's story went something like this:

Christopher, a magnificent giant, left home in search of the most powerful king in the world so that he could serve him. On his travels, he first met a great Christian king and pledged to follow him. One day, a jester entertained the royal court with a song about the devil. And every time the king heard the word *devil*, he made the sign of the cross. Puzzled by this strange gesture, Christopher asked the king what it meant. "Whenever I hear the devil mentioned," said the king, "I defend myself with this sign for fear that he might get some power over me and do me harm."

"If you are afraid of the devil," said Christopher, "he must be stronger and greater than you. So, goodbye! I am going to look for the devil and enter his service because he must be the most powerful king on earth."

A short time later, as Christopher was walking along a road, he met a large army. Their leader, a formidable-looking warrior in black armor, asked him where he was going. Christopher said, "I'm searching for the devil. I want to take him as my master."

"I'm the one you're looking for," said the warrior. Glad to have found the devil, Christopher promised to serve him and joined his army. As the army continued their march, they passed a roadside cross. When the devil noticed it, he was terrified and hid behind a boulder. Shocked by his new master's behavior, Christopher asked him what made him so afraid. The devil hemmed and hawed, refusing to answer, but Christopher insisted. So the devil relented and said, "Once a man named Jesus Christ was nailed to a cross, and when I see his sign, it fills me with terror, and I run from it."

"If that's the case," said Christopher, "then this Jesus is greater and more powerful than you. Therefore, I still haven't found the greatest king on earth. So I'm leaving you. I'm going to search for Christ and make him my master."

Later in the story, Christopher finds Christ while working as a ferryman to carry people across a river. And he takes Christ as his king and serves him until his martyrdom.[3]

The Devil's Defeat

Today, centuries after St. Christopher's time, the sign of the cross has not lost any of its power over Satan. He still cowers and turns tail at the sight of it. So making the sign still protects us from our most dangerous enemy. But here's the funny thing. Even though the sign of the cross assures our victory in our battles with the devil, we don't use it very much. It is a mighty, surefire weapon right at hand, but we ignore it.

Why don't we take advantage of this powerful weapon? I think the reason has to do with our attitude toward the devil. Many people just don't have him on their radar screen. They believe the devil exists, but with their eyes fixed on everyday things, they don't pay him any attention. Others don't believe the devil exists and so don't see that an enemy lurks about waiting to snare them. Neither of these two groups use the sign as an instrument of spiritual warfare because they do not realize that they are at war.

But we are embroiled in a war with the devil, and the stakes are high because our salvation is at risk. The devil's very name signals our great danger. One of the Greek words used for the devil is *diabolos*, which means "throw across." The devil throws himself across God's plan to rescue us from sin and death, attempting to block it.

Jesus himself spoke clearly about Satan's threat to

humankind. He said that the devil was "a murderer from the start" and "a liar, and the father of lies" (John 8:44). He declared that his purpose in life was to redeem all humanity from Satan's grip by submitting to death on the cross. He said, "Now the prince of this world is to be driven out. And when I am lifted up from the earth, I shall draw all people to myself" (John 12:31–32).

Christ's victory on the cross came as a complete surprise to the devil. He had expected that he would win it all by taking the life of God's Son. Satan did have a claim against human beings insofar as we had given ourselves over to his service through sin. He knew that because of our sins we had a debt to pay that would cost us our lives. But he made a huge mistake by attempting to claim the life of Christ, the sinless one against whom he had no claim at all. Instead of the cross achieving the devil's great design to destroy Jesus, it cost him his control over all humanity.

The Fathers of the Church taught that if Satan realized what God intended to accomplish for us in Christ, he would never have pursued the Crucifixion. For instance, listen to St. Leo the Great (d. 461), who was the pope in the mid-fifth century:

> That God might deliver humanity from the bonds of the death-bringing transgression, he concealed the power of Christ's majesty from the fury of the devil (see 1 Cor. 2:8), and offered him instead the infirmity of our lowliness. For had this proud and cruel enemy known the plan of God's mercy, he would have striven rather to temper with mildness the hearts of [those who crucified

Christ] rather than to inflame them with evil hate, so that he might not lose the slavery of all his captives, while he pursued the liberty of the one who owed him nothing.

And so his own wickedness tricked him. He inflicted a torment on the Son of God that was changed into a medicine for all of the sons of men. He shed innocent blood, which became both the price and the drink that restored the world. The Lord . . . suffered upon himself the wicked hands of those who raged against him, who while intent on their crime yet served the plan of the Redeemer.[4]

So on that day nearly two thousand years ago, the cross became Satan's ruin and from that time its sign has paralyzed him with fear.

Applying Christ's Victory

Christ handed on to us the victory of his cross at our Baptism (see chapter four). The sacrament included one or more exorcisms in which the celebrant signed us with the cross while he commanded the devil to depart from us. He also asked us to renounce Satan, which we did ourselves if we were baptized as adults or which our parents and godparents did in our name if we were baptized as infants.

God then used the waters of Baptism to immerse us into the mystery of the cross itself. In the sacramental bath, we died with Christ and rose with him to a new life. At that pivotal moment, the Lord marked us with the sign of the cross, the seal that claimed us as belonging to him.

The Fathers of the Church taught that God stamped us with the sign of the cross to make us inviolable. With it he guarantees our safety by warning the enemy not to harm or even to touch us. "The invocation of grace," said St. Cyril of Jerusalem about Baptism, "marking your soul with its seal prevents the terrible demon from swallowing you up."[5]

Our baptismal seal of inviolability equips us for victory in our daily battles with the devil. We engage its defensive and offensive properties each time we sign ourselves. The sign of the cross reminds the devil that we are Christ's possession and he dare not injure us. And it repels him because the gesture invokes the painful memory of his defeat.

Now here's a puzzle that may be bothering you, but it's only an apparent problem. If Christ conquered Satan on the cross, why is he still a threat to us? Why, for example, does St. Peter warn us that our "enemy the devil is on the prowl like a *roaring lion*, looking for someone to devour" (1 Pet. 5:8; emphasis added)? If Jesus defeated him, why is he still free to roam around and cause us trouble?

An illustration from World War II casts some light on our situation with Satan. Although the war did not end until the summer of 1945, the victory of the Allies in Europe was assured in 1943. In that year, factories in the United States began to produce more planes and ships than the Axis powers were destroying. Final victory was only a matter of time. The rest of the European campaign was one big mop-up operation.

Similarly, Christ won the war with Satan on the cross, but Satan has not yet left the field. Christ wanted us to participate in his great work of redemption, so he engaged us to perform the mop-up operation. We, the members of the Church, the Body of Christ, have the privilege of enforcing the Lord's triumph over the devil. The tables are turned, and the intended victims of Satan's onslaught have become his conquerors.

So until Jesus comes again, we will have to fight skirmishes with the devil. No doubt about it, he is a dangerous adversary. Yet we must never forget that the Lord has given us the upper hand: he has won the war. But we must apply his victory in our daily lives. Like St. Christopher, we must take the Lord as our master and, armed with his holy sign, join him in battle against our mutual enemy.

CHAPTER EIGHT
A Victory Over Self-Indulgence

All who belong to Christ Jesus have crucified self with all its passions and its desires. Since we are living in the Spirit, let our behavior be guided by the Spirit and let us not be conceited or provocative or envious of one another.

—GALATIANS 5:24–26

We must expect the cure of all our wounds from the sign of the cross. If the venom of avarice courses through our veins, let's make the sign of the cross, and the venom will be expelled. If the scorpion of sensuality stings us, let's use the same means, and we shall be healed. If the basest of worldly thoughts seek to defile us, let's again make the sign of the cross, and we shall live the divine life.[1]

—ST. MAXIMUS OF TURIN (c. 380–c. 423)

You have stripped off your old behavior with your old self, and you have put on a new self which will progress toward true knowledge the more it is renewed in the image of its Creator.

—COLOSSIANS 3:9–10

✝

I have had lifelong problems with anger, impatience, and criticalness, to name a few of my troublesome flaws. Trapped in wrongdoing arranged by one of them, my occasional first thought is to blame someone else. *If Adam hadn't blown it in the Garden*, I think, *maybe I wouldn't have blown my stack!* Or closer to home, I imagine that I caught my anger, like a virus, from my feisty Italian-American mother. Think about your problems. Do you struggle with anger, as I do? Or jealousy, or sensuality, or laziness, or addictions, or some other bad behavior? Like me, do you sometimes blame them on someone else? Maybe on Adam and Eve or your mom and dad?

Such excuses contain germs of truth. Original sin and family patterns affect our conduct. But the real origin of unruly behavior is within ourselves. From the heart. That's where Jesus located the source of our sinful problems. "From the heart," he said, "come evil intentions: murder, adultery, fornication, theft, perjury, slander" (Matt. 15:19). To this list he could well have added, among many others, the famous seven deadly sins that we struggle with: pride, wrath, envy, sloth, gluttony, greed, and lust.

Scripture calls this root cause of our problems "the flesh." For example, St. Paul says, "The works of the flesh are plain: fornication, impurity, licentiousness, idolatry, sorcery, enmity, strife, jealousy, anger, selfishness, dissension, party spirit, envy, drunkenness, carousing, and the like" (Gal. 5:19 RSV). I prefer the term *self-indulgence*, because to the sex-saturated contemporary mind, the word *flesh* suggests that the body or sexuality instigates our problems, which is not what Scripture is saying. Rather, the Bible points to a force within that seduces us to sin.

We cozy up to our self-indulgence because it licenses bad things that we like to do. We also pretend that because of its influence, we cannot stop committing our favorite sins. I used to think that I just could not prevent myself from occasionally exploding with rage. I have learned that this was a convenient lie that permitted me to hang on to my pet wrongdoing. The truth is that the Lord confers on us in Baptism the power to deal effectively with our self-indulgence. In that sacrament, he frees us by the power of his cross so that we no longer have to obey the siren song of sin. In Baptism, he also gives us the sign of the cross as a means of curbing our evil tendencies. I think you will agree that it is a very practical tool. Let's take a look at what the sign can do to our self-indulgence.

Crucifying Our Base Desires

We can deal with problems that stem from our evil tendencies in one of two ways. We can either give in to them or fight them. Neither way is easy because both hurt. Giving in to bad behaviors causes pain for us and for the people we love. And fighting sinful problems hurts because it requires us to kill our self-indulgence.

So when we decide that we want to get free from a problem, we have a fight on our hands. We are taking sides against self-indulgence in its war against the Spirit that we received in Baptism. "The desires of self-indulgence," said St. Paul, "are always in opposition to the Spirit and the desires of the Spirit are in opposition to self-indulgence" (Gal. 5:17). Our strategy in this spiritual warfare is killing self-indulgence by saying no to the evil behaviors that it promotes. "You must kill everything in you that is earthly," said St. Paul, "sexual vice, impurity, uncontrolled passion, especially greed. . . . You must also give up all these things: human anger, hot temper, malice, abusive language, and dirty talk" (Col. 3:5–6, 8).

When we engage this battle against self-indulgence, we can expect to go at it for a long time. We do not have a silver bullet that will put it to death instantly with a single shot. Scripture says that we must crucify our self-indulgence, and crucifixion is a slow, agonizing form of death: "All who belong to Christ Jesus," said St. Paul, "have crucified self with all its passions and its desires" (Gal. 5:24). And we can employ the sign of the cross as a most appropriate instrument for this purpose.

We can declare our opposition to our evil tendencies every morning with the sign of the cross. While making the gesture, we can say something like "Lord, today, by the power of your cross, I refuse to give in to my problem with envy"—or whatever behavior bedevils you. If you were a fly on the wall in my living room during my prayer time, you might witness me signing myself and saying, "Lord, I put to death on this cross my anger. Give me the strength to say no to it today."

The *today* is a very important part of such prayers. We can readily resist our self-indulgence one day at a time. But if we were to declare that we would never again yield to anger, envy, or any other evil impulse, we may soon find ourselves defeated and discouraged. The *never* in such a statement foolishly creates an opportunity for self-indulgence to ambush us. Never is a very long time, and imagining that we were safe, we would soon lower our defenses. But daily vigilance empowered by the cross assures our ultimate victory.

So first thing in the morning, we refuse our evil tendencies with the sign of the cross. Then during the day we can sign ourselves to combat self-indulgence when it lures us to our favorite wrongdoing. The great Christian writers have always maintained confidence in the power of the sign to neutralize such temptations. "Who is the man," asked St. Bernard of Clairvaux (1090–1153), "so completely master of his thoughts as never to have impure ones? But it is necessary to repress their attacks immediately so that we may vanquish the enemy where he hoped to triumph. The infallible means of success is to make the sign of the cross."[2] And Origen summed up the role of the sign of the cross in our overcoming self-indulgence: "Such is the power of the sign of the cross that if we place it before our eyes, if we keep it faithfully in our heart, neither concupiscence, nor sensuality, nor anger can resist it. At its appearance the whole army of self-indulgence and sin take to flight."[3]

Clothing Ourselves with Christ

But our victory over self-indulgence would not be complete if we merely eliminated our bad behaviors. We must learn to replace our anger, meanness, sensuality, and the like with their opposites. And the sign of the cross, just as it helps us conquer our evil desires, can also aid us in acquiring virtuous character traits like patience, kindness, and chastity.

As we have seen, our Baptism is a radical, life-changing event. In it, by the power of his cross, Christ frees us from sin and death and gives us a new, supernatural life. We shed our old sinful nature at the baptismal font and put on a new nature that is fashioned in the Lord's own image. "You have stripped off your old behavior with your old self," said St. Paul, "and you have put on a new self which will progress toward true knowledge the more it is renewed in the image of its Creator" (Col. 3:9–10). This passage contains both a surprising truth and suggests a practical tool for Christian growth.

First, the surprising truth. The new self that we get in Baptism is not a finished product. God is going to renew us progressively in his own image. The first time I read the above quote in Colossians, I said, "Whoa!" Then I hit my brain's rewind button, and I read the passage over and over again. The fact that the Lord intended to remake me to be like himself startled and delighted me.

So, in Baptism we put on a new nature that God continues to develop and perfect. Our transformation is the work of the Holy Spirit, who replicates Christ's character in us and enables us to behave as he did when he lived on earth. Scripture calls these characteristics of Christ the *fruit of the Spirit* and lists them as love, joy, peace, patience, kindness, goodness, faithfulness, gentleness, self-control (see Gal. 5:22–23 RSV). Each fruit of the Spirit allows us to replace a bad behavior with a good one. We substitute love for hate, peace for enmity, restraint for rage, and so on.

The practical tool suggested by Colossians 3 is a way to use the sign of the cross to help us replace evil conduct by adopting Christ's behaviors. Let me give you some background before I tell you how it works.

The text employs the analogy of stripping off old clothes and putting on new ones to describe our transformation in Christ. The Fathers of the Church developed this theme, teaching that stripping off our old nature in Baptism and putting on a new one was a participation in Christ's stripping at his Crucifixion. And in the early Church, candidates for Baptism were stripped before their immersion just as Christ was stripped at the cross. Addressing newly baptized Christians, St. Cyril of Jerusalem said:

> When you entered the baptistery, you took off your clothes as an image of putting off the old man with his deeds. Having stripped naked, you were also imitating Christ, who was stripped naked on the cross. And by his nakedness he put off from himself the principalities and powers . . . triumphing over them in the cross." Since the evil powers once made their lair in your members, you may no longer wear that old clothing.

I am not speaking of your visible body, but the "old nature . . . corrupt through deceitful lusts."[4]

As the newly baptized Christians emerged from the pool, they put on white garments, symbolizing that they had risen to a new life and put on Christ, who was clothed in glory at his Resurrection. "Everyone of you that has been baptized," said St. Paul, "has been clothed in Christ" (Gal. 3:27).

By now you have probably anticipated how making the sign of the cross comes into play. We can regard it as our way of participating in Christ's stripping at the Crucifixion and his being clothed with glory at his Resurrection. And we can use it to engage the grace of Baptism to help us substitute the fruit of the Spirit for works of self-indulgence. We can trace the cross over our bodies while praying, "Lord, with this sign, I strip off my evil tendencies, the residues of my old nature that still cling to me." Then we can sign ourselves again, praying, "O Holy Spirit, with this cross, I put on Christ and ask you to help me live as he did."

When I do this, I get very specific. "Lord," I say as I cross myself, "in your name, I strip off like dirty clothes my anger, my impatience, and my criticalness." Then I sign myself a second time, saying, "Lord, with this cross, I put on Christ's restraint, his patience, and his compassion."

If my family and friends were to overhear me at these moments, they would breathe a great sigh of relief.

CONCLUSION
Graces and Choices

Whene'er across this sinful flesh of mine
*   I draw the Holy Sign,*
All good thoughts stir within me, and renew
*   Their slumbering strength divine;*
Till there springs up a courage high and true
*   To suffer and to do.*[1]

—ST. JOHN HENRY NEWMAN (1801–1890)

If you bear on your forehead the sign of the humility of Jesus
Christ, bear in your heart the imitation of the humility of Jesus
Christ.[2]

—ST. AUGUSTINE (354–430)

✝

Blessed Maria Assunta Pallotta (1878–1905), a simple girl from a poor Italian family, said that she joined the convent in order to become a saint. Her community, the Franciscan Missionaries of Mary, assigned her to work in the kitchen and on the farm. In 1904, they sent Maria Assunta to serve at their mission in China. On the way, she and her companions stopped at Bombay, India, and she wrote the following in a letter to her sisters back home:

> We saw four of these poor people bowing down in worship before a large stone painted red, and then dabbing their foreheads with some of the red varnish. I thought how they could put to shame some of us Christians who are so filled with human respect that we cannot even make the sign of the cross openly.[3]

I earnestly desire that Maria Assunta's words will never apply to me or to any of you, my readers. I hope that as a result of reading this book, you have felt freer to make the sign of the cross openly. Yes, I hope that you are imitating your Christian ancestors and are signing yourself first thing in the morning and last thing at night, when you eat and drink, when you leave the house and when you return, when you are walking, driving, riding a bus, or flying, at home, at school, at work, or at leisure. I hope, too, for those of you that are parents, that you are using the sign to bless your children. In short, I hope you have begun to make the sign in all circumstances, as the Fathers of the Church—cited often in this book—prescribed.

We have been exploring the realities invoked by the sign of the cross. We have studied them as a way of recovering the power of the ancient prayer. Review them with me here so that they may be etched in your memory and available at your fingertips:

By making the sign of the cross, you:

1) Open yourself to God by confessing your faith in the Blessed Trinity and basic Christian doctrines. Assure that you are praying to the God who created you, not to one that you created. Call on God's name as a way of entering his presence and praying with Godpower.

2) Choose to live the supernatural life you received when you died and rose with Christ at your Baptism. Hold yourself to the fact that you have died to sin and so refuse to yield to it. Acknowledge your membership in the Body of Christ and expect the Holy Spirit to flow in you afresh.

3) Affirm your decision to be Christ's disciple. Deny that you belong to yourself. Declare that all that you are and have belong to the Lord. Decide to follow him by embracing his teaching and obeying his commandments.

4) Accept suffering as a normal part of the Christian life. Realize that the Lord stays with you and supports you in your suffering. Embrace hardship and pain as a way of participating in Christ's suffering and of winning spiritual advantages for others.

5) Repel the devil by reminding him of Christ's victory. Eliminate his attempts to harm you by joining Christ's battle and resisting him. Claim the inviolability from spiritual enemies that is yours since you belong to Christ.

6) Kill your self-indulgence and evil tendencies to sin. Strip off your old sinful nature and its bad behavior. Clothe yourself with your new nature that the Lord is renewing in his image. Acquire the fruit of the Spirit.

Each time you make the sign of the cross, you engage these realities. Occasionally, as you sign yourself, you may be especially aware of one or more of them—for example, remembering your Baptism or your discipleship. Sometimes you may choose to focus specifically on just one of them—for example, accepting a hardship or refusing a temptation. But most of the time, you cross yourself without thinking about any of these specifics. To reprise a main theme of this book, you must never make the sign of the cross casually or carelessly, but must always make it reverently and with faith.

Now as we are about to bring our exploration to a close, I hope that you agree with my claim that making the sign of the cross is an easy spiritual discipline. What could be easier than touching your forehead, breast, and shoulders while praying in the Lord's name? You have right at hand a simple gesture and prayer that opens you to a tremendous flow of graces. The sign is an act of faith that engages God's love for you and the spiritual power that he wants to release in you.

But you have also discovered in these pages that the sign of the cross sums up your Christian life and vocation, and because of that, it is not so easy. It calls you to affirm hard choices, decisions that you have made at great personal cost. Making the sign says that you are holding yourself to these choices, and in doing so you are joining Christ at the cross. You are crucifying all the things that oppose the decisions you have made to embrace God's will. That's hard to do. But you have a stream of grace to support and sustain you in this effort.

So the sign of the cross opens us to graces that enable us to affirm our choices. With St. John Henry Newman, we draw the holy sign across our sinful flesh "till there springs up a courage high and true / to suffer and to do." That's God's grace. With St. Augustine, we mark our foreheads with the sign of Christ's humility so that in our hearts we might truly imitate his humility in holding fast to the decisions we have made, subordinating our will to God's will. That's our choice.

And like Blessed Maria Assunta, making the sign of the cross freely, we just may become saints.

BIBLIOGRAPHY

Ante-Nicene Fathers: The Writings of the Fathers Down to A.D. 325. Christian Classics Ethereal Library. www.ccel.org.

Catechism of the Catholic Church. 2nd ed. Vatican City: Libreria Editrice Vaticana, 1997.

Danielou, Jean, SJ. *The Bible and the Liturgy.* Ann Arbor, MI: Servant Books, 1979.

Primitive Christian Symbols. London: Burns & Oates, 1964.

Gaume, Jean-Joseph. *The Sign of the Cross in the Nineteenth Century.* Philadelphia: Peter F. Cunningham, 1873.

Lambing, A.A. *The Sacramentals of the Holy Catholic Church.* New York: Benziger Brothers, 1892.

Lewis, C.S. *The Screwtape Letters.* New York: Bantam Books, 1982.

Nicene and Post-Nicene Fathers. Christian Classics Ethereal Library. www.ccel.org.

O'Connor, Edward D., CSC. *The Catholic Vision.* Huntington, Indiana: Our Sunday Visitor, 1992.

Richardson, Alan, ed. *A Theological Word Book of the Bible.* New York: Macmillan Publishing Company, 1950.

Sheed, F.J. *Theology and Sanity.* San Francisco: Ignatius Press, 1993.

Thurston, Herbert. *Familiar Prayers: Their Origin and History.* Westminster, MD: The Newman Press, 1953.

Thurston, Herbert, "Sign of the Cross," in *The Catholic Encyclopedia*, vol. 13, 785–787. New York: The Universal Knowledge Foundation, Inc., 1907.

NOTES

Epigraph

1. Quoted in Jean-Joseph Gaume, *The Sign of the Cross in the Nineteenth Century* (Philadelphia: Peter F. Cunningham, 1873), 25.

Chapter One: Recovering the Power of the Ancient Sign

1. Quoted in A.A. Lambing, *The Sacramentals of the Holy Catholic Church* (New York: Benziger Brothers, 1892), 63.

2. Quoted in Lambing, *The Sacramentals*, 75.

3. Various internet sites carry this story. See, for example, Luke Veronis, "The Sign of the Cross," at http://www.incommunion.org/ Cross.htm.

4. Quoted in Herbert Thurston, "The Sign of the Cross," *The Catholic Encyclopedia*, vol. 13 (New York: Universal Knowledge Foundation, 1907), 786. Cited hereafter as *CE*.

5. Quoted in Lambing, *The Sacramentals*, 75.

6. *Catechism of the Catholic Church*, 2nd ed. (Vatican City: Libreria Editrice Vaticana, 1997), no. 1670. Cited hereafter as *CCC*.

Chapter Two: A Short History of the Sign of the Cross

1. *CE*, 786–7.

2. *Luther's Little Instruction Book (The Small Catechism of Martin Luther)*, trans. Robert E. Smith, Project Wittenberg, May 22, 1994, http://www.projectwittenberg.org/pub/resources/text/wittenberg/ luther/little.book/web/book-appx.html.

3. *Saint Caesarius of Arles: Sermons*, vol. 1, trans. Sr. Mary Magdeleine Mueller, OSF, The Fathers of the Church: A New Translation, vol. 31 (Washington, DC: The Catholic University of America Press, 1956), 75.

4. In Jean Danielou, SJ, *The Bible and the Liturgy* (Ann Arbor, Michigan: Servant Books, 1979), 64.

5. Adapted from a citation in Herbert Thurston, *Familiar Prayers: Their Origin and History* (Westminster, MD: Newman, 1953), 2.

6. *CE*, 789.

7. Thurston, *Familiar Prayers*, 3.

8. *CE*, 786.

Chapter Three: An Opening to God

1. Quoted in Gaume, *The Sign of the Cross in the Nineteenth Century*, 323.

2. *Roman Missal* © 2010. International Commission on English in the Liturgy Corporation.

3. C.S. Lewis, *The Screwtape Letters* (New York: Macmillan, 1982), 11–12.

Chapter Four: A Renewal of Baptism

1. Quoted in Sr. Athanasius Braegelmann, *The Life and Writings of Saint Ildefonsus of Toledo* (Washington, DC: The Catholic University of America Press, 1942), 79.

2. Quoted in Danielou, *The Bible and the Liturgy*, 61.

3. Quoted in Danielou, *The Bible and the Liturgy*, 61 (emphasis added).

4. See *CCC*, nos. 1262–65.

5. St. Cyril of Jerusalem, *Catechetical Lectures* 20.4, in Nicene and Post-Nicene Fathers, series 2, vol. 7 (Edinburgh: T&T Clark, 1893), Christian Classics Ethereal Library, www.ccel.org (adapted for readability). Cited hereafter as NPNF.

6. Quoted in Braegelmann, *Life and Writings of Saint Ildefonsus*, 79.

Chapter Five: A Mark of Discipleship

1. Quoted in Gaume, *The Sign of the Cross in the Nineteenth Century*, 321.

2. "Prayer of Saint Richard of Chichester," Loyola Press, https://www.loyolapress.com/catholic-resources/prayer/traditional-catholic-prayers/saints-prayers/day-by-day-prayer-of-saint-richard-of-chichester/.

3. St. Cyril of Jerusalem, *Catechetical Lectures* 1.2, in NPNF, series 2, vol. 7 (adapted for readability).

4. St. Gregory Nazianzen, "The Oration on Holy Baptism," in NPNF, series 2, vol. 7 (adapted for readability).

5. Quoted in Danielou, *The Bible and the Liturgy*, 59.

6. For more clarity of thought on the Lord's ownership of us, see Letter 21 in C.S. Lewis, *The Screwtape Letters*.

7. See *Vatican Council II: The Conciliar and Post Conciliar Documents*, rev. ed., ed. Austin Flannery, OP (Northport, NY: Costello, 1992).

8. F.J. Sheed, *Theology and Sanity* (San Francisco: Ignatius, 1993); Edward D. O'Connor, CSC, *The Catholic Vision* (Huntington, IN: Our Sunday Visitor, 1992).

9. Sheed, *Theology and Sanity*, 7, 22–30.

Chapter Six: An Acceptance of Suffering

1. Lactantius, The Divine Institutes 4.26, in Ante-Nicene Fathers: The Writings of the Fathers Down to A.D. 325, vol. 7, ed. Alexander Roberts and James Donaldson (Edinburgh: T&T Clark, 1885), Christian Classics Ethereal Library, www.ccel.org.

2. In Lucy Menzies, *Mirrors of the Holy* (London: A. R. Mowbray & Co., 1928), 303 and 305.

Chapter Seven: A Defense Against the Devil

1. St. Cyril of Jerusalem, *Catechetical Lectures* 13.36, in NPNF, series 2, vol. 7 (adapted for readability).

2. Quoted in Lambing, *The Sacramentals*, 63.

3. See the St. Christopher legend in various editions of *The Golden Legend* by Jacob of Voragine (c. 1230–c. 1298).

4. *The Roman Breviary*, trans. John Patrick Crichton-Stuart (Edinburgh/London: William Blackwood and Sons, 1908), 2, 352–3.

5. St. Cyril of Jerusalem, *Catechetical Lectures* 3.12, in NPNF, series 2, vol. 7 (adapted for readability).

Chapter Eight: A Victory Over Self-Indulgence

1. Quoted in Lambing, *The Sacramentals*, 65-6.

2. Quoted in Lambing, *The Sacramentals*, 66.

3. Quoted in Lambing, *The Sacramentals*, 62.

4. St. Cyril of Jerusalem, *Catechetical Lectures* 20.2, in *NPNF*, series 2, vol. 7 (adapted for readability).

Conclusion: Graces and Choices

1. St. John Henry Newman, "The Sign of the Cross," in *Verses on Various Occasions* (London: Longmans, 1903), 69, www.newmanreader.org.

2. Quoted in Gaume, *The Sign of the Cross in the Nineteenth Century*, 324.

3. *The Theme Song of Assunta*, compiled by one of her sisters (N. Providence, RI: Franciscan Missionaries of Mary, 1956), 122.